OUR
JUST THE FACTS

A Short and Concise Guide to
Our Life, Estate, and Wishes

....
NAME & DATE

....
NAME & DATE

CONFIDENTIAL

This portfolio contains confidential information
and should be stored in a safe place.

Published by 55 Plus ES, LLC
www.55PlusES.com
Copyright © 2025 Susan Loumagne

Author: Susan Loumagne

ISBN: 979-8-9867618-7-9

This book is not a legal document nor is it a Will.
No liability is assumed for losses or damages due to the information provided.

All rights reserved. No portion of this book may be reproduced in any form without permission
from the publisher, except as permitted by U.S. copyright law.
For permissions contact: *info@55pluses.com*

TABLE OF CONTENTS

Welcome Page 5

Quick Start Guide 6

Resources 7

    Useful listings for replacement of important documents, government resources, and support organizations

To-Do Notes 8

    Use these pages to track what you need to do, find, or replace

SECTION ONE

Personal Profile and Important Contacts....(pages for two people)...... 10

    Parents, siblings, children, employment, volunteerism, military service, and storage of important papers

Finances...(pages for two people) 20

    Banking, credit cards, personal income, financial advisor and investments, insurance policies – life, property, auto, health, dental, and tax records

Assets...(pages for two people) 32

    Real estate – home, investment, and vacation, property tax declarations, storage of keys, garage door code, hidden assets, vehicles, loans given, and personal property

Monthly Bills, Subscriptions, and Giving 38

    Record your obligations for household bills and recurring payments

Pet Information 41

    Name, type of pet, veterinarian, medications, vaccines, microchip status, pet insurance, notable markings, health conditions, and your pet care service.

SECTIONS TWO AND THREE
Dedicated section for each person

Person One Pages 44-62   Person Two Pages 63-86

Medical and Medications.. 45 | 64

> Doctors, medical conditions, medical equipment, vision, allergies, vaccines, and medications

I I'm Unable to Communicate...49 | 67

> A list of what to do and who to contact.

Estate and Legal Documents...50 | 68

> Will, executor, power of attorney, and healthcare directives

Passwords..52 | 70

> Cell phone, computer, websites, and social media,

Thoughts, Words, and Wishes..54 | 72

> Take the opportunity to share your thoughts. What motivates you in life? The words you live by? Wishes for the future?

Final Wishes...55 | 73

> Designation of your final disposition, viewing, obituary, graveside, . military honors, service, and reception

Additional Information...58 |76

> Use this section to record information about pets, a business, partnership, investments, or anything you haven't shared in any other section.

Letters to Loved Ones *(two for each person)*............................59 |77

WELCOME TO OUR JUST THE FACTS

- **Designed for Two** – *Dedicated pages for each person to complete individually.*

- **Purpose** – *Capture key estate and personal details to assist loved ones in case of illness, incapacity, or passing.*

- **If You Lack a Will or Healthcare Directive** – *Use the Resources section to get started. Inform loved ones where this guide is stored and discuss your wishes with family or an attorney.*

How to Use This Guide

- *Complete only relevant sections.*

- *Use To-Do Notes to track updates, missing info, or documents to locate.*

- *Review & update your Will, insurance, and other coverages.*

- *Inform loved ones where this guide is stored and discuss key decisions.*

Feedback & Resources

- *Leave a review on Amazon – Your feedback is appreciated!*

- *Visit THE STORE at www.55pluses.com for companion items and additional Portfolios.*

This planner is not a legal document and cannot be considered a Will or any other legal document.

QUICK START GUIDE TO COMPLETING OUR JUST THE FACTS PORTFOLIO

1: Schedule It

Block off time this week to begin your Guide. At the end of the session, schedule the next time you will work on the next sections.

2: Do it

You may want to work with a partner. One person writes while the other dictates the information. Only fill in the information you feel comfortable adding. For example, you may want to use only the last 4 digits of your Social Security number or credit card account.

3: To-Do List

Use the To-Do page to keep a list of what information and documents you need to find, copy, or replace.

4: Photo and Video It

Take photos of your family and pets for identification purposes. In addition, take photos and videos of your home's contents and exterior, so you'll have a visual record for yourself and insurance claims.

5. Follow Up

Order copies of missing documents and complete all lingering tasks on your list. The Resource Page has links to help you obtain originals of any essential missing cards or documents.

6: Store It

We recommend storing this Guide with your essential legal and estate documents, photos, letters to loved ones, and other necessary and important items you've referenced. It's wise to purchase a fireproof and waterproof lock box with a one-hour (minimum) fireproof rating to store these items.

7: Share It

Let trusted people know that you have this Guide and where it is stored. It is also the perfect time to initiate hard-to-have conversations to discuss your estate and let people know your wishes.

8: Update It

Schedule a time a year from now to update your information.

RESOURCES

Vital Records

Birth, Death, Marriage, and Divorce Records   www.cdc.gov/nchs/w2w.htm
Link to your state's Bureau of Vital Statistics

Government Programs

Medicare   www.medicare.gov
800-633-4227

Social Security Office   www.socialsecurity.gov
800-772-1213

Veterans Administration   www.va.gov
800-827-1000

Veterans Service Records National Archives   www.archives.gov/veterans
866-272-6272

Passports – U.S. Passports   www.travel.state.gov
877-487-2778

Estate and Must Have Documents

Wills, Healthcare Directives, and Durable Power of Attorney

National Academy of Elder Law Attorneys   www.naela.org
703-942-5711

Legal Zoom   www.legalzoom.com
800-773-0888

Emergency Preparation & Disaster Relief

American Red Cross   www.redcross.org
800-733-2767

FEMA – Federal Emergency Management Association   www.fema.gov
800-621-3362

Ready.gov   www.ready.gov
800-621-3362

TO DO NOTES

.REMINDER: Set-up a reminder to review and update this Portfolio yearly..............

TO DO NOTES

PERSONAL PROFILE PERSON ONE

Name: ....

Birth Date: .... Place of Birth: ....

Name on Birth Certificate: ....

Mother's Maiden Name: .... Living? ....

....

Father's Name: .... Living? ....

....

Relationship Status: .... Spouse/Partner's Name: ....

....

Employed By: ....

Job Title: ....

Supervisor's Name and Phone Number: ....

....

Volunteer Organizations and Contacts:. ....

....

....

Military Branch: .... Rank: ....

Dates Served and Where? ....

....

NOTES ....

....

....

....

IMPORTANT PAPERS - Person One

Examples of important papers are social security card, birth certificate, passport, driver's license, military DD214, marriage license, divorce record, resident alien card, adoption record, frequent traveler #.

Type	Number	Stored Where?	Copy Y/N

CHILDREN - Person One

Name of Parents: ....

Social Security Number Optional

Given Name: ....

Date of Birth: .... Place of Birth: ....

SS#: .... Phone Number: ....

Email: ....

Given Name: ....

Date of Birth: .... Place of Birth: ....

SS#: .... Phone Number: ....

Email: ....

Given Name: ....

Date of Birth: .... Place of Birth: ....

SS#: .... Phone Number: ....

Email: ....

Given Name: ....

Date of Birth: .... Place of Birth: ....

SS#: .... Phone Number: ....

Email: ....

Given Name: ....

Date of Birth: .... Place of Birth: ....

SS#: .... Phone Number: ....

Email: ....

SIBLINGS - Person One

Name: .... Birth Date: ....

Phone: .... Living?: ....

Email or Address: ....

Name: .... Birth Date: ....

Phone: .... Living?: ....

Email or Address: ....

Name: .... Birth Date: ....

Phone: .... Living?: ....

Email or Address: ....

Name: .... Birth Date: ....

Phone: .... Living?: ....

Email or Address: ....

Name: .... Birth Date: ....

Phone: .... Living?: ....

Email or Address: ....

Name: .... Birth Date: ....

Phone: .... Living?: ....

Email or Address: ....

PERSONAL PROFILE PERSON TWO

Name: ....

Birth Date: .... Place of Birth: ....

Name on Birth Certificate: ....

Mother's Maiden Name: .... Living? ....

....

Father's Name: .... Living? ....

....

Relationship Status: .... Spouse/Partner's Name: ....

....

Employed By: ....

Job Title: ....

Supervisor's Name and Phone Number: ....

....

Volunteer Organizations and Contacts: . ...

....

....

Military Branch: .... Rank: ....

Dates Served and Where? ....

....

NOTES ....

....

....

....

IMPORTANT PAPERS - Person Two

Examples of important papers are social security card, birth certificate, passport, driver's license, military DD214, marriage license, divorce record, resident alien card, adoption record, frequent traveler #.

Type	Number	Stored Where?	Copy Y/N

CHILDREN - Person Two

Name of Parents: ....

Social Security Number Optional

Given Name: ....

Date of Birth: .... Place of Birth: ....

SS#: .... Phone Number: ....

Email: ....

Given Name: ....

Date of Birth: .... Place of Birth: ....

SS#: .... Phone Number: ....

Email: ....

Given Name: ....

Date of Birth: .... Place of Birth: ....

SS#: .... Phone Number: ....

Email: ....

Given Name: ....

Date of Birth: .... Place of Birth: ....

SS#: .... Phone Number: ....

Email: ....

Given Name: ....

Date of Birth: .... Place of Birth: ....

SS#: .... Phone Number: ....

Email: ....

SIBLINGS - Person Two

Name: .... Birth Date: ....

Phone: .... Living?: ....

Email or Address: ....

Name: .... Birth Date: ....

Phone: .... Living?: ....

Email or Address: ....

Name: .... Birth Date: ....

Phone: .... Living?: ....

Email or Address: ....

Name: .... Birth Date: ....

Phone: .... Living?: ....

Email or Address: ....

Name: .... Birth Date: ....

Phone: .... Living?: ....

Email or Address: ....

Name: .... Birth Date: ....

Phone: .... Living?: ....

Email or Address: ....

IMPORTANT CONTACTS

Name: .... Relationship: ....

Phone: .... Phone: ....

Email or Address: ....

Name: .... Relationship: ....

Phone: .... Phone: ....

Email or Address: ....

Name: .... Relationship: ....

Phone: .... Phone: ....

Email or Address: ....

Name: .... Relationship: ....

Phone: .... Phone: ....

Email or Address: ....

Name: .... Relationship: ....

Phone: .... Phone: ....

Email or Address: ....

Name: .... Relationship: ....

Phone: .... Phone: ....

Email or Address: ....

IMPORTANT CONTACTS

Name: .... Relationship: ....

Phone: .... Phone: ....

Email or Address: ....

___

Name: .... Relationship: ....

Phone: .... Phone: ....

Email or Address: ....

___

Name: .... Relationship: ....

Phone: .... Phone: ....

Email or Address: ....

___

Name: .... Relationship: ....

Phone: .... Phone: ....

Email or Address: ....

___

Name: .... Relationship: ....

Phone: .... Phone: ....

Email or Address: ....

___

Name: .... Relationship: ....

Phone: .... Phone: ....

Email or Address: ....

FINANCES

BANKING *Add log-in information to Password Section*

Name of Bank: ....

Branch Location: ....

Contact's Name: .... Phone No: ....

Account Type	Account Number * optional	Name on Account

Notes: ....

Name of Bank: ....

Branch Location: ....

Contact's Name: .... Phone No: ....

Account Type	Account Number * optional	Name on Account

Notes: ....

Name of Bank: ....

Branch Location: ....

Contact's Name: .... Phone No: ....

Account Type	Account Number * optional	Name on Account

Notes: ....

CREDIT CARDS

* Account number and security code optional. Add log-in information to the Passwords Section.

Name of Company: .... Phone No: ....

Name on Account: ....

Account Number: .... Security Code: ....

Expiration: .... Balance Insured: ....

Name of Company: .... Phone No: ....

Name on Account: ....

Account Number: .... Security Code: ....

Expiration: .... Balance Insured: ....

Name of Company: .... Phone No: ....

Name on Account: ....

Account Number: .... Security Code: ....

Expiration: .... Balance Insured: ....

Name of Company: .... Phone No: ....

Name on Account: ....

Account Number: .... Security Code: ....

Expiration: .... Balance Insured: ....

Name of Company: .... Phone No: ....

Name on Account: ....

Account Number: .... Security Code: ....

Expiration: .... Balance Insured: ....

CREDIT CARDS

Account number and security code optional. Add log-in information to the Passwords Section.

Name of Company: .... Phone No: ....

Name on Account: ....

Account Number: .... Security Code: ....

Expiration: .... Balance Insured: ....

Name of Company: .... Phone No: ....

Name on Account: ....

Account Number: .... Security Code: ....

Expiration: .... Balance Insured: ....

Name of Company: .... Phone No: ....

Name on Account: ....

Account Number: .... Security Code: ....

Expiration: .... Balance Insured: ....

Name of Company: .... Phone No: ....

Name on Account: ....

Account Number: .... Security Code: ....

Expiration: .... Balance Insured: ....

Name of Company: .... Phone No: ....

Name on Account: ....

Account Number: .... Security Code: ....

Expiration: .... Balance Insured: ....

FINANCIAL SERVICES and CD'S

Company Name: ....

Advisor's Name: .... Phone Number: ....

Email: ....

Notes: ....

....

Company Name: ....

Advisor's Name: .... Phone Number: ....

Email: ....

Notes: ....

....

CERTIFICATE OF DEPOSIT

Bank: ....

Amount: .... Interest Rate: .... Maturity Date: ....

Bank: ....

Amount: .... Interest Rate: .... Maturity Date: ....

Bank: ....

Amount: .... Interest Rate: .... Maturity Date: ....

Bank: ....

Amount: .... Interest Rate: .... Maturity Date: ....

SAVINGS BONDS STORAGE

....

....

....

INVESTMENTS

Name: ....

Investment Type: .... * 401K, IRA, Mutual Funds, Stocks, Crypto, NFTs
Held By: .... Phone Number: ....
Account Number: ....
Notes:..
....

Investment Type: .... * 401K, IRA, Mutual Funds, Stocks, Crypto, NFTs
Held By: .... Phone Number: ....
Account Number: ....
Notes:..
....

Investment Type: .... * 401K, IRA, Mutual Funds, Stocks, Crypto, NFTs
Held By: .... Phone Number: ....
Account Number: ....
Notes:..
....

Investment Type: .... * 401K, IRA, Mutual Funds, Stocks, Crypto, NFTs
Held By: .... Phone Number: ....
Account Number: ....
Notes:..
....

Investment Type: .... * 401K, IRA, Mutual Funds, Stocks, Crypto, NFTs
Held By: .... Phone Number: ....
Account Number: ....
Notes:..
....

PERSONAL INCOME - Person One

This section covers any income you receive, such as salary, social security, pensions, annuities, military, trusts, royalties, bonuses, dividends, interest, alimony, or any other income.

Type:* ....
Company: .... Phone: ....
Amount: .... Note: ....

Type:* ....
Company: .... Phone: ....
Amount: .... Note: ....

Type:* ....
Company: .... Phone: ....
Amount: .... Note: ....

Type:* ....
Company: .... Phone: ....
Amount: .... Note: ....

Type:* ....
Company: .... Phone: ....
Amount: .... Note: ....

Type:* ....
Company: .... Phone: ....
Amount: .... Note: ....

Type:* ....
Company: .... Phone: ....
Amount: .... Note: ....

PERSONAL INCOME - Person Two

This section covers any income you receive, such as salary, social security, pensions, annuities, military, trusts, royalties, bonuses, dividends, interest, alimony, or any other income.

Type:* ....
Company: .... Phone: ....
Amount: .... Note: ....

Type:* ....
Company: .... Phone: ....
Amount: .... Note: ....

Type:* ....
Company: .... Phone: ....
Amount: .... Note: ....

Type:* ....
Company: .... Phone: ....
Amount: .... Note: ....

Type:* ....
Company: .... Phone: ....
Amount: .... Note: ....

Type:* ....
Company: .... Phone: ....
Amount: .... Note: ....

Type:* ....
Company: .... Phone: ....
Amount: .... Note: ....

LOANS YOU OWE

Loan From: .... Phone: ....
Account Number: ....
Type of Loan: .... Interest Rate: ....
Amount: .... Payment: ....
Date of Origination: .... Length of Loan: ....

Loan From: .... Phone: ....
Account Number: ....
Type of Loan: .... Interest Rate: ....
Amount: .... Payment: ....
Date of Origination: .... Length of Loan: ....

Loan From: .... Phone: ....
Account Number: ....
Type of Loan: .... Interest Rate: ....
Amount: .... Payment: ....
Date of Origination: .... Length of Loan: ....

Loan From: .... Phone: ....
Account Number: ....
Type of Loan: .... Interest Rate: ....
Amount: .... Payment: ....
Date of Origination: .... Length of Loan: ....

Loan From: .... Phone: ....
Account Number: ....
Type of Loan: .... Interest Rate: ....
Amount: .... Payment: ....
Date of Origination: .... Length of Loan: ....

INSURANCE

AUTO INSURANCE - *Vehicle, make, model, Vin# is also in the Assets section.*

Company: .... Phone: ....

Policy Number: .... Policy Stored Where? ....

Agent Name: .... Agent Phone: ....

Company: .... Phone: ....

Policy Number: .... Policy Stored Where? ....

Agent Name: .... Agent Phone: ....

HEALTH, DENTAL, AND PRESCRIPTION INSURANCE

Name on Policy: ....

Company: .... Phone: ....

Policy Number: .... Policy Stored Where? ....

Coverage: ....

Notes: ....

....

Name on Policy: ....

Company: .... Phone: ....

Policy Number: .... Policy Stored Where? ....

Coverage: ....

Notes: ....

....

Name on Policy: ....

Company: .... Phone: ....

Policy Number: .... Policy Stored Where? ....

Coverage: ....

Notes: ....

LIFE INSURANCE

Name on Policy: ....

Company: .... Phone Number: ....

Agent: .... Phone Number: ....

Policy Number: .... Policy Stored Where? ....

Amount: .... Whole Life or Term: .... Length of Policy: ....

Notes: ....

Beneficiary Name: .... Phone Number: ....

Beneficiary Address: .... Aware of Designation? ....

Contingent Name: .... Phone Number: ....

Name on Policy: ....

Company: .... Phone Number: ....

Agent: .... Phone Number: ....

Policy Number: .... Policy Stored Where? ....

Amount: .... Whole Life or Term: .... Length of Policy: ....

Notes: ....

Beneficiary Name: .... Phone Number: ....

Beneficiary Address: .... Aware of Designation? ....

Contingent Name: .... Phone Number: ....

Do you have other employee/retiree supplemental life insurance plans?

Plan Name: ....

Details: ....

Do you have other employee/retiree supplemental life insurance plans?

Plan Name: ....

Details: ....

ADDITIONAL INSURANCE

Type: ....
Company: .... Amount: ....
Policy Number: .... Stored? ....
Agent Name: .... Phone Number: ....
Notes: ....

Type: ....
Company: .... Amount: ....
Policy Number: .... Stored? ....
Agent Name: .... Phone Number: ....
Notes: ....

Type: ....
Company: .... Amount: ....
Policy Number: .... Stored? ....
Agent Name: .... Phone Number: ....
Notes: ....

Type: ....
Company: .... Amount: ....
Policy Number: .... Stored? ....
Agent Name: .... Phone Number: ....
Notes: ....

Type: ....
Company: .... Amount: ....
Policy Number: .... Stored? ....
Agent Name: .... Phone Number: ....
Notes: ....

INCOME TAX FILING

Where do you store previous years' tax returns? ....

Do you use an online service to complete and file your taxes? ....

Online service information: ....
....

Accountant's name and email: ....

Notes: ....

ADDITIONAL FINANCIAL INFORMATION

Notes: ....
....
....
....
....
....
....
....
....
....
....
....
....
....
....
....
....
....
....
....
....
....
....

ASSETS

REAL ESTATE

Property Type: .... Home, Investment, Rental, Vacation

Address: ....

Purchase Date: .... Payment: ....

Mortgage Held By: ....

Balance of Loan: .... As of date: ....

Value of Property: .... As of date: ....

Homeowners Insurance Company: ....

Property Taxes - **Amount and how are they paid?:** ....

Property Type: .... Home, Investment, Rental, Vacation

Address: ....

Purchase Date: .... Payment: ....

Mortgage Held By: ....

Balance of Loan: .... As of date: ....

Value of Property: .... As of date: ....

Homeowners Insurance Company: ....

Property Taxes - **Amount and how are they paid?**...

Property Type: .... Home, Investment, Rental, Vacation

Address: ....

Purchase Date: .... Payment: ....

Mortgage Held By: ....

Balance of Loan: .... As of date: ....

Value of Property: .... As of date: ....

Homeowners Insurance Company: ....

Property Taxes - **Amount and how are they paid?**...

STORAGE OF CODES, KEYS AND PROPERTY

Garage Door Code:............................ Security System Code:................................

Where do you keep extra keys for your house, and cars? ....

....

....

Do you have a Storage Unit? Details: ....

....

DOCUMENT AND VALUABLES STORAGE

Do you have a fireproof lock box? Where is the key or what is the code? ....
....

Do you have a safe deposit box?   Where is the key or what is the code? ....

....

STORED ASSETS

Don't let your hidden assets be lost forever. Include information about any secret locations here. Or, write down the details and store them in a safety deposit or lock box to protect your assets.

Do you have assets hidden in your home?   Y/N Where? ....

Does anyone else know the location? Y/N If yes, who? ....

If no one else knows, you should share the location or an obvious hint.

Location or hint? ....

....

Do you have assets stored in another location?   Y/N Where? ....

Does anyone else know the location? Y/N If yes, who? ....

If no one else knows, you should share the location or give an obvious hint.

Location or hint? ....

....

VEHICLES

Vehicle Type: .... * Automobile, Boat, Motor home, Motorcycle, Truck

Make: .... Model: .... Year: ....

Registered To: .... VIN#: ....

Status of Ownership: .... Title Stored? ....

Vehicle Type: .... * Automobile, Boat, Motor home, Motorcycle, Truck

Make: .... Model: .... Year: ....

Registered To: .... VIN#: ....

Status of Ownership: .... Title Stored? ....

Vehicle Type: .... * Automobile, Boat, Motor home, Motorcycle, Truck

Make: .... Model: .... Year: ....

Registered To: .... VIN#: ....

Status of Ownership: .... Title Stored? ....

Vehicle Type: .... * Automobile, Boat, Motor home, Motorcycle, Truck

Make: .... Model: .... Year: ....

Registered To: .... VIN#: ....

Status of Ownership: .... Title Stored? ....

Vehicle Type: .... * Automobile, Boat, Motor home, Motorcycle, Truck

Make: .... Model: .... Year: ....

Registered To: .... VIN#: ....

Status of Ownership: .... Title Stored? ....

LOAN AGREEMENTS - Money you are owed

The following are loans that you have given to other people or companies.

To Whom: .... Amount: ....

Contact Information: ....

What are the details of the loan and where is the Promissory Note?

....

To Whom: .... Amount: ....

Contact Information: ....

What are the details of the loan and where is the Promissory Note?

....

To Whom: .... Amount: ....

Contact Information: ....

What are the details of the loan and where is the Promissory Note?

....

ADDITIONAL INFORMATION ABOUT ASSETS

....
....
....
....
....
....
....
....
....
....
....

PERSONAL PROPERTY

This section covers different categories of items, such as jewelry, coins, firearms, artwork, collectibles, etc. We recommend you have your items appraised and obtain the proper insurance to cover them in case of loss due to theft, flood, fire, or natural disaster.

Category Name: ....

Have you had any of the items appraised?   Y/N

Do you have an insurance rider on any of these items?   Y/N

Do you have videos or photographs of any or all of these items?   Y/N

Where are the photos and/or videos stored? ....

Notes or list items: ....

....

....

....

....

Category Name: ....

Have you had any of the items appraised?   Y/N

Do you have an insurance rider on any of these items?   Y/N

Do you have videos or photographs of any or all of these items? Y/N

Where are the photos and/or videos stored? ....

Notes or list items: ....

....

....

....

....

PERSONAL PROPERTY

Category Name: ....

Have you had any of the items appraised?   Y/N

Do you have an insurance rider on any of these items?   Y/N

Do you have videos or photographs of any or all of these items? Y/N

Where are the photos and/or videos stored? ....

Notes or list items:...

....

....

....

....

....

Use additional pages to list more items.

....

....

....

....

....

....

....

....

....

....

....

....

MONTHLY BILLS

Company: .... Phone number: ....
Account number: .... Contact name: ....
Bill received by mail or email: ....
What address: ....
How do you pay? .... *Check, Website, Auto-Debit
How often do you pay? .... What amount? ....
*Full, Minimum, Other

Company: .... Phone number: ....
Account number: .... Contact name: ....
Bill received by mail or email: ....
What address: ....
How do you pay? .... *Check, Website, Auto-Debit
How often do you pay? .... What amount? ....
*Full, Minimum, Other

Company: .... Phone number: ....
Account number: .... Contact name: ....
Bill received by mail or email: ....
What address: ....
How do you pay? .... *Check, Website, Auto-Debit
How often do you pay? .... What amount? ....
*Full, Minimum, Other

Company: .... Phone number: ....
Account number: .... Contact name: ....
Bill received by mail or email: ....
What address: ....
How do you pay? .... *Check, Website, Auto-Debit
How often do you pay? .... What amount? ....

MONTHLY BILLS

Company: .... Phone number: ....

Account number: .... Contact name: ....

Bill received by mail or email: ....

What address: ....

How do you pay? .... *Check, Website, Auto-Debit

How often do you pay? .... What amount? ....

*Full, Minimum, Other

Company: .... Phone number: ....

Account number: .... Contact name: ....

Bill received by mail or email: ....

What address: ....

How do you pay? .... *Check, Website, Auto-Debit

How often do you pay? .... What amount? ....

*Full, Minimum, Other

Company: .... Phone number: ....

Account number: .... Contact name: ....

Bill received by mail or email: ....

What address: ....

How do you pay? .... *Check, Website, Auto-Debit

How often do you pay? .... What amount? ....

*Full, Minimum, Other

If you have additional monthly bills, write them on a separate sheet of paper and store them inside this book.

SUBSCRIPTIONS, MEMBERSHIPS, AND PUBLICATIONS

Make a list of all your online and print accounts with dues or payments. You may add log-in information here or on the password page.

....
....
....
....
....
....
....
....
....
....
....
....
....
....
....
....
....
....
....
....
....
....
....
....
....
....
....

PET INFORMATION

Pet Name: .... Date of Birth: .... Age: ....

Breed: .... Coat Color: ....

☐ Canine/Dog ☐ Feline/Cat ☐ Neutered or Spayed Other: ....

Notable markings on pet: ....

Veterinarian name and phone number: ....
....

24-hour Veterinarian name and phone number: ....
....

Is this a service animal with certification? ....

Where do you keep the certification document? ....

Any Medical or Behavioral Alerts? Seizures, caution with humans or other animals, adverse reactions to medications, allergies, blindness, deafness, etc.

....
....

IDENTIFICATION

Does your pet have identification tags with your name and phone number? Y/N

What name and number are on the tags? ....
....

Does your pet have a microchip or tattoo? ....
....

What is the number? ....
....
....

Local shelter name and phone number: ....
....

PET VACCINES

Common Vaccines: Bordetella, Lepto, DHPP, DHLPP, Rattlesnake, FVRCP, Feline Leukemia

Where do you keep the vaccine records? ....

Date of Last Rabies Vaccine: ....

Name of Vaccine: .... Date: ....

Name of Vaccine: .... Date: ....

Name of Vaccine: .... Date: ....

Name of Vaccine: .... Date: ....

Name of Vaccine: .... Date: ....

Name of Vaccine: .... Date: ....

MEDICATIONS

Is your pet on medications? ....

Name of medications: ....

....

Where do you purchase the medications? ....

....

If online, what is the website and account information? ....

....

Account User ID: .... Password: ....

Are your orders on auto-delivery? ....

....

Additional notes: ....

....

PET INSURANCE

Do you have a pet insurance? ....
....

What is the company name and policy number? ....
....
....

PET CARE SERVICE

List the name of the people or companies you use for: walking, feeding, or overnights.

Name: .... Phone Number: ....

Name: .... Phone Number: ....

LONG-TERM CARE PLANNING

Have you designated someone to care for your pet if you are unable? ....

Name and contact information: ....
....

Details of the arrangement: ....
....
....
....

Have you done estate planning for your pet and included it as part of your Will? ....

Details of the arrangement: ....
....
....
....

Additional notes about your pet: ....
....

PERSON ONE

MEDICAL INFORMATION - PERSON ONE

Name: .... Date ....

Blood Type .... Height .... Weight ....

DOCTORS *(General Practitioner, Specialists, Audiology, Internist, Cardiologist)*

Doctor: .... Specialty: ....

Phone: ....

Doctor: .... Specialty: ....

Phone: ....

Doctor: .... Specialty: ....

Phone: ....

Doctor: .... Specialty: ....

Phone: ....

* PATIENT PORTAL INFORMATION – add to PASSWORDS

Veterans Administration Facility: .... Phone: ....

....

DENTAL and VISION

Dentist: .... Phone: ....

Eye Doctor: .... Phone: ....

Where do you buy your contact lenses? ....

Where do you buy your glasses? ....

VACCINES Do you get a yearly flu shot? ....

Have you had the shingles or pneumonia vaccines? ....

MEDICAL CONDITIONS

Do you have any medical conditions that require monitoring? ....

....

Do you have any hereditary conditions or risk factors? ....

....

MEDICATIONS

Do you take any life sustaining medications? List them here and on your Medications Form

....

....

Are you allergic to any medications? ....

....

MEDICAL EQUIPMENT

Do you use medical equipment? ....

Who is the supplier? .... Phone: ....

Details: ....

....

ALLERGIES

Do you have additional allergies? List your allergy medications here and on your Medications Form.

....

....

....

MEDICATIONS - PERSON ONE

Name: .... Pharmacy: ....

Drug Allergies: ....

Drug Name	Treatment of	Started Taking	Dosage	How Often is the Drug Taken?	Prescribed by Whom?

MEDICATIONS - PERSON ONE

Name: .... Pharmacy: ....

Drug Allergies: ....

Drug Name	Treatment of	Started Taking	Dosage	How Often is the Drug Taken?	Prescribed by Whom?

IF I'M UNABLE TO COMMUNICATE,

please take care of the following items: **ONE**

ESTATE & LEGAL DOCUMENTS
WILL, TRUST, AND POA - PERSON ONE

My attorney is: .... Phone: ....

WILL

An attorney can help you draft and update your Will to ensure your estate is distributed according to your wishes and to minimize potential tax burdens. Regularly review and update your Will to reflect changes in your family, assets, and legal requirements. Online services can also help to create a will.

Attorney who handled the Will: .... Phone: ....
At the law firm of: ....
Last Will is dated: ....
The executor/executrix is: ....
Are they aware they are the executor? ....
Have you discussed the Will with them? ....
*Remind your executor to request multiple copies of your death certificate for accessing your accounts.

Will is stored: .... A copy is stored: ....
Notes: ....
....

ESTABLISHING A TRUST

It may be appropriate to seek your attorney's and financial advisor's advice to determine if establishing a trust fund would benefit your situation.

Title of the trust ....

Trustees and contact information: ....
....
....

DURABLE FINANCIAL POWER OF ATTORNEY

A Durable Financial Power of Attorney allows a designated Agent to manage your financial affairs if you become unable to do so, even temporarily. You can specify which powers your Agent may exercise. This authority ends upon your death, at which point your executor assumes responsibility.

Do you have a financial POA? .... Effective when? ....
Name of your Agent? ....

Where is your financial POA stored? ....

LIVING WILL AND HEALTH CARE POWER OF ATTORNEY

A Living Will outlines your medical treatment preferences if you cannot communicate. A Health Care Power of Attorney designates someone to make healthcare decisions for you. Share copies with your agent, family, doctors, and attorney. Check whether your Living Will allows copies or requires originals.

LIVING WILL OR MEDICAL DIRECTIVE

Do you have a Living Will Declaration?................. Effective when?... ....

Do you a DNR? ....

To carry out my Living Will, I designate: ....

Have you discussed your wishes with them? ....

The alternate agent is: ....

My Living Will has been given to: ....

Copies are stored:: ....

HEALTH CARE POWER OF ATTORNEY

Do you have a Health Care Power of Attorney? ....

Effective when? ....

I designate as my Health Care Power of Attorney: ....

Have you discussed your wishes with them? ....

The alternate agent is: ....

My Health Care Directive has been given to: ....

Copies are stored:: ....

ORGAN DONATION

I do............................ I do not............................ want any of my organs donated.

I want only the following organs donated: ....
....

Notes:...
....

PASSWORDS

Name: ....

Company / Site Address	User ID	Password
Cell Phone 1		
Computer		

PASSWORDS

Name: ....

Company / Site Address	User ID	Password
Cell Phone 1		
Computer		

THOUGHTS, WORDS, AND WISHES ONE

FINAL WISHES - PERSON ONE

DESIGNATIONS

Do you want to designate someone to carry out your wishes for your funeral? Y/N

If yes, who and have you discussed your wishes with them? ....

Do you have money set aside for your funeral? If yes, where? ....

....

What is your choice for the final disposition of your body?

Burial-traditional in-ground: ....   Burial-above ground: ....

Burial-green: ....   Cremation-traditional: ....

Placement of cremation ashes? ....

....

RELIGIOUS OR MEMORIAL SERVICE

Type of Service: ....   Location: ....

Officiant Name: ....   Phone Number: ....

FUNERAL HOME

Funeral Home Preference: ....

Contact Name: ....   Phone Number: ....

Have you purchased a package from the funeral home? Y/N

CEMETERY

Cemetery Name: ....

I have a plot in the name of: ....   The deed is stored: ....

I am entitled to military honors: Y/N   I am entitled to Veteran's benefits: Y/N

NOTES: ....

....

....

VIEWING - ONE
If there is a casket, would you like a viewing? ....
....

OBITUARY
Would you like to write your Obituary, or is there something you want to be mentioned in your Obituary? If so, write it on a separate sheet and add it to the end of the book.

SERVICE
Would you like a religious service or a memorial service?
....
Where would you like the service to be held?
....
Please describe the mood or tone of the service you'd like to have.
....
What hymns or music would you like to be played?
....
Which Bible verses, poetry, or readings would you like to have read?
....
Who would you like to speak?
....
Do you have photos or other remembrances that you'd like displayed? Please describe.
....
Would you like to specify a charity in place of flowers?
....
Would you like to give your guests something at the service, such as a program, memorial card, photograph, or bookmark?
....
Please identify specific people, if any, that you want to be sure are invited to your service.
....
....
....
....
....

MILITARY HONORS - ONE

If you are entitled to military honors, a flag presentation, and playing "Taps," would you like to have the benefits? ....

GRAVESIDE

Would you like everyone to be invited to the graveside? ....

Have you purchased a headstone? ....

What type of headstone would you like to have, and what would you like engraved on it? ....
....

Would you like to specify a special reading? ....

Is there someone you would like to speak? ....
....

Would you like people to place something on your casket? ....

RECEPTION

Where would you like the reception to be held? ....
....

Who would you like to be invited? ....
....
....

POST-RECEPTION ACTIVITY

Would you like your friends and loved ones to do something together or individually to honor you? (Ideas: a memorial scholarship, taking a walk, stories, etc.
....
....

Additional wishes and thoughts:
....
....
....
....

ADDITIONAL INFORMATION - ONE

Include anything that is not covered in any other section.

LETTER TO A LOVED ONE - #1

LETTER TO A LOVED ONE - #1

LETTER TO A LOVED ONE - #2

LETTER TO A LOVED ONE - #2

PERSON TWO

MEDICAL INFORMATION - PERSON TWO

Name: .... Date ....

Blood Type .... Height .... Weight ....

DOCTORS *(General Practitioner, Specialists, Audiology, Internist, Cardiologists)*

Doctor: .... Specialty: ....

Phone: ....

Doctor: .... Specialty: ....

Phone: ....

Doctor: .... Specialty: ....

Phone: ....

Doctor: .... Specialty: ....

Phone: ....

* PATIENT PORTAL INFORMATION – add to PASSWORDS

Veterans Administration Facility: .... Phone: ....

....

DENTAL and VISION

Dentist: .... Phone: ....

Eye Doctor: .... Phone: ....

Where do you buy your contact lenses? ....

Where do you buy your glasses? ....

VACCINES Do you get a yearly flu shot? ....

Have you had the shingles or pneumonia vaccines? ....

MEDICAL CONDITIONS

Do you have any medical conditions that require monitoring? ....

....

Do you have any hereditary conditions or risk factors? ....

....

MEDICATIONS

Do you take any life sustaining medications? List them here and on your Medications Form

....

....

Are you allergic to any medications? ....

....

MEDICAL EQUIPMENT

Do you use medical equipment? ....

Who is the supplier? .... Phone: ....

Details: ....

....

ALLERGIES

Do you have additional allergies? List your allergy medications here and on your Medications Form.

....

....

MEDICATIONS - PERSON TWO

Name: .... Pharmacy: ....
Drug Allergies: ....

Drug Name	Treatment of	Started Taking	Dosage	How Often is the Drug Taken?	Prescribed by Whom?

IF I'M UNABLE TO COMMUNICATE,
please take care of the following items: **TWO**

ESTATE & LEGAL DOCUMENTS
WILL, TRUST, AND POA - PERSON TWO

My attorney is: .... Phone: ....

WILL

An attorney can help you draft and update your Will to ensure your estate is distributed according to your wishes and to minimize potential tax burdens. Regularly review and update your Will to reflect changes in your family, assets, and legal requirements. Online services can also help to create a will.

Attorney who handled the Will: .... Phone: ....
At the law firm of: ....
Last Will is dated: ....
The executor/executrix is: ....
Are they aware they are the executor? ....
Have you discussed the Will with them? ....
Remind your executor to request multiple copies of your death certificate for accessing your accounts.

Will is stored: .... A copy is stored: ....
Notes:...
....

ESTABLISHING A TRUST

Title of the trust ....

Trustees and contact information: ....
....
....

DURABLE FINANCIAL POWER OF ATTORNEY

A Durable Financial Power of Attorney allows a designated Agent to manage your financial affairs if you become unable to do so, even temporarily. You can specify which powers your Agent may exercise. This authority ends upon your death, at which point your executor assumes responsibility.

Do you have a financial POA? .... Effective when? ....

Name of your Agent? ....

Where is your financial POA stored? ....

LIVING WILL AND HEALTH CARE POWER OF ATTORNEY

A Living Will outlines your medical treatment preferences if you cannot communicate. A Health Care Power of Attorney designates someone to make healthcare decisions for you. Share copies with your agent, family, doctors, and attorney. Check whether your Living Will allows copies or requires originals.

LIVING WILL OR MEDICAL DIRECTIVE

Do you have a Living Will Declaration?................. Effective when?... ....

Do you a DNR? ....

To carry out my Living Will, I designate: ....

Have you discussed your wishes with them? ....

The alternate agent is: ....

My Living Will has been given to: ....

Copies are stored:: ....

HEALTH CARE POWER OF ATTORNEY

Do you have a Health Care Power of Attorney? ....

Effective when? ....

I designate as my Health Care Power of Attorney: ....

Have you discussed your wishes with them? ....

The alternate agent is: ....

My Health Care Directive has been given to: ....

Copies are stored:: ....

ORGAN DONATION

I do........................... I do not........................... want any of my organs donated.

I want only the following organs donated: ....

....

Notes:..

....

PASSWORDS

Name: ....

Company / Site Address	User ID	Password
Cell Phone 1		
Computer		

PASSWORDS

Name: ....

Company / Site Address	User ID	Password
Cell Phone		
Computer		

THOUGHTS, WORDS, AND WISHES - TWO

FINAL WISHES - PERSON TWO

DESIGNATIONS

Do you want to designate someone to carry out your wishes for your funeral? Y/N

If yes, who and have you discussed your wishes with them? ....

Do you have money set aside for your funeral? If yes, where? ....

....

What is your choice for the final disposition of your body?

Burial-traditional in-ground: .... Burial-above ground: ....

Burial-green: .... Cremation-traditional: ....

Placement of cremation ashes? ....

....

RELIGIOUS OR MEMORIAL SERVICE

Type of Service: .... Location: ....

Officiant Name: .... Phone Number: ....

FUNERAL HOME

Funeral Home Preference: ....

Contact Name: .... Phone Number: ....

Have you purchased a package from the funeral home? Y/N

CEMETERY

Cemetery Name: ....

I have a plot in the name of: .... The deed is stored: ....

I am entitled to military honors: Y/N   I am entitled to Veteran's benefits: Y/N

NOTES: ....

....

....

....

VIEWING - TWO

If there is a casket, would you like a viewing? ....
....

OBITUARY

Would you like to write your Obituary, or is there something you want to be mentioned in your Obituary? If so, write it on a separate sheet and add it to the end of the book.

SERVICE

Would you like a religious service or a memorial service?
....
Where would you like the service to be held?
....
Please describe the mood or tone of the service you'd like to have.
....
What hymns or music would you like to be played?
....
Which Bible verses, poetry, or readings would you like to have read?
....
Who would you like to speak?
....
Do you have photos or other remembrances that you'd like displayed? Please describe.
....
Would you like to specify a charity in place of flowers?
....
Would you like to give your guests something at the service, such as a program, memorial card, photograph, or bookmark?
....
Please identify specific people, if any, that you want to be sure are invited to your service.
....
....
....
....
....

MILITARY HONORS - TWO

If you are entitled to military honors, a flag presentation, and playing "Taps," would you like to have the benefits? ....

GRAVESIDE

Would you like everyone to be invited to the graveside? ....

Have you purchased a headstone? ....

What type of headstone would you like to have, and what would you like engraved on it? ....
....

Would you like to specify a special reading? ....

Is there someone you would like to speak? ....
....

Would you like people to place something on your casket? ....

RECEPTION

Where would you like the reception to be held? ....
....

Who would you like to be invited? ....
....
....

POST-RECEPTION ACTIVITY

Would you like your friends and loved ones to do something together or individually to honor you? (Ideas: a memorial scholarship, taking a walk, stories, etc.
....
....

Additional wishes and thoughts:
....
....
....
....

ADDITIONAL INFORMATION - *PERSON TWO*

Include anything that is not covered in any other section.

LETTER TO A LOVED ONE - #1

LETTER TO A LOVED ONE - #1

LETTER TO A LOVED ONE - #2

LETTER TO A LOVED ONE - #2